MOUNTAIN BIKES

Janet Cook

Consultants: **Al Heubach and Geoff Apps**

Designed by **Mary Forster**

Additional designs by **Ruth Strohl-Palmer**

Cover design by **Stephen Wright**

Illustrated by **Kim Raymond** and **Kuo Kang Chen**

Photographs taken on location in California
by **Mike Powell, Allsport USA**

Additional photographs by **Otto Greule, Jr.** and **W.L. Gillingham**

This book was produced in association with **MUDDY FOX** 🐾

Contents

2

Using this book

This book covers all you need to know to become a competent rider, from efficient gear-changing and braking to such advanced skills as bunny-hopping and ditch-jumping.

Budding competitors can find out about events such as observed trials and downhill races. There are tips on how to prepare for a competition and do your best on the day.

Emergency repair panels cover some mechanical problems you may encounter *en-route*. At the back of the book there is advice on cleaning and maintaining your bike.

Safety first

You can greatly reduce the chances of being seriously injured in a bicycling accident if you ride cautiously and use your common sense. In addition to this, you should always wear a helmet.

Your head is the most sensitive part of your body. Wearing a helmet could prevent concussion, brain damage, or death.

Helmets needn't be uncomfortable. Modern designs are light and well-ventilated.

Mountain bike etiquette

Unfortunately, mountain biking has been given a bad name by a few thoughtless riders who have shown little care for the countryside or other users. It is therefore important that riders work together to earn back respect for the sport. Without the support of landowners, ramblers, horseriders and so on, tracks open to mountain bikes could become very limited.

Remember:
* Give way to other countryside users.
* Don't drop litter.
* Close gates behind you.
* Be polite and courteous.
* As you approach animals, slow down and give them a wide berth.
* Don't take unnecessary risks.
* Don't be too noisy.
* Don't create a fire hazard.
* Don't skid unnecessarily.

About mountain bikes

Mountain bikes are tough. When ridden skilfully, they can go through ditches and potholes, cope with water and mud, climb near-vertical slopes, and bring you downhill with control and stability.

The picture below shows all the mountain bike parts, and tells you what they are called. If you are thinking about buying a bike yourself, go to pages 32-33 for advice.

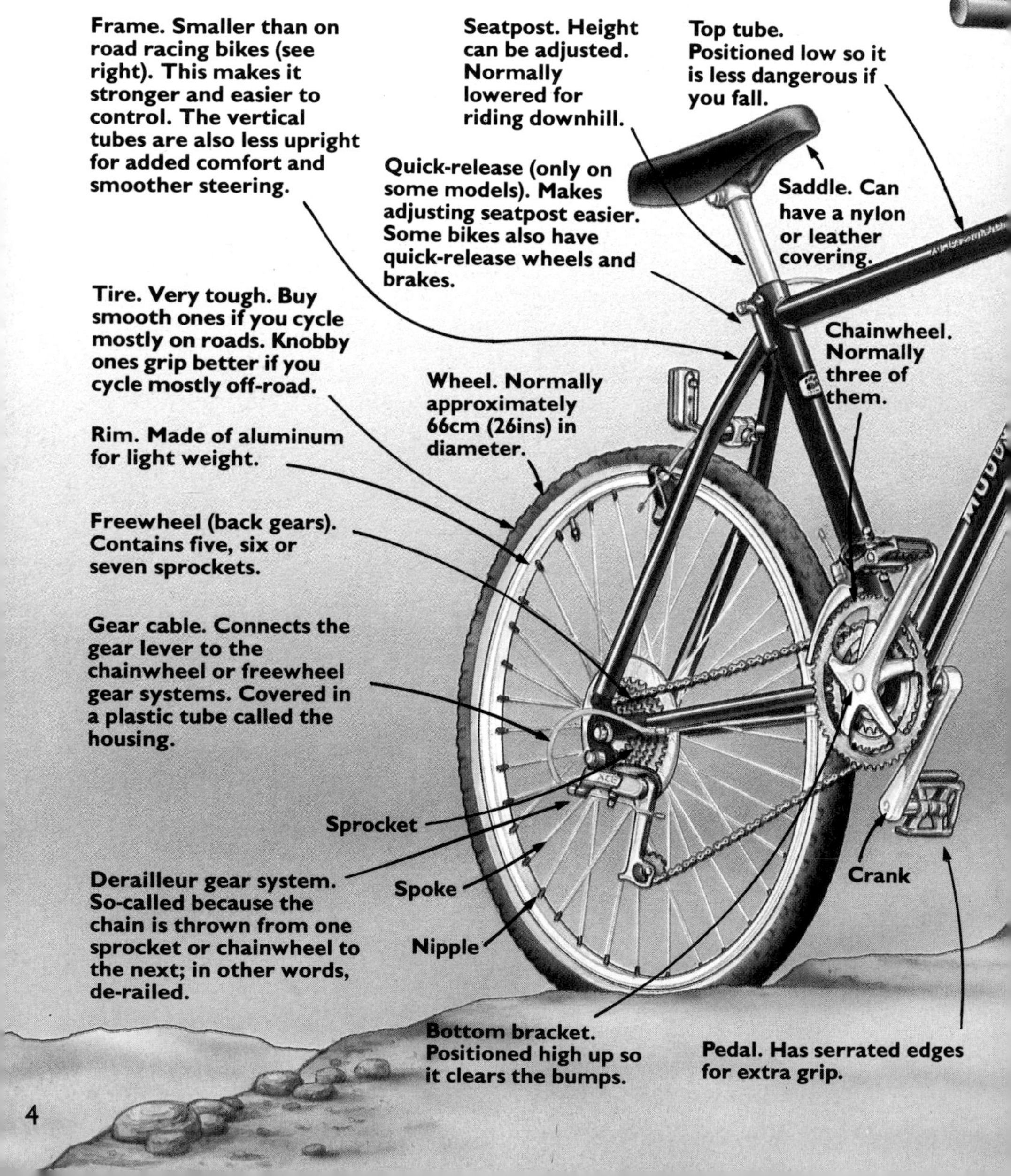

Frame. Smaller than on road racing bikes (see right). This makes it stronger and easier to control. The vertical tubes are also less upright for added comfort and smoother steering.

Seatpost. Height can be adjusted. Normally lowered for riding downhill.

Top tube. Positioned low so it is less dangerous if you fall.

Quick-release (only on some models). Makes adjusting seatpost easier. Some bikes also have quick-release wheels and brakes.

Saddle. Can have a nylon or leather covering.

Tire. Very tough. Buy smooth ones if you cycle mostly on roads. Knobby ones grip better if you cycle mostly off-road.

Chainwheel. Normally three of them.

Wheel. Normally approximately 66cm (26ins) in diameter.

Rim. Made of aluminum for light weight.

Freewheel (back gears). Contains five, six or seven sprockets.

Gear cable. Connects the gear lever to the chainwheel or freewheel gear systems. Covered in a plastic tube called the housing.

Sprocket

Derailleur gear system. So-called because the chain is thrown from one sprocket or chainwheel to the next; in other words, de-railed.

Spoke

Nipple

Crank

Bottom bracket. Positioned high up so it clears the bumps.

Pedal. Has serrated edges for extra grip.

Handlebars.
Normally a flat
design, with a
slight curve.

Gear lever.
Positioned so that
you can change
gear with your
thumb.

Brake. Types vary,
but cantilever
brakes are most
common; they are
strong and easy to
maintain.

Grip

**Handlebar
stem**

Brake block

Hub. Supports the
wheel, holds the
spokes, and carries
the bearing around
which the wheel
revolves.

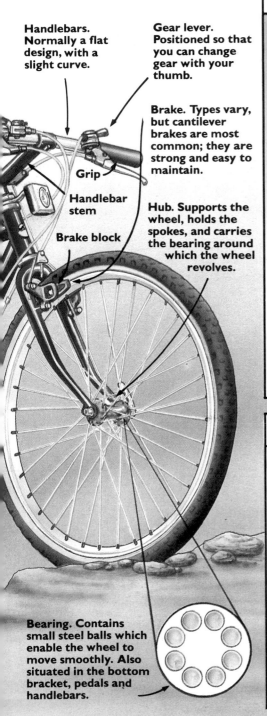

**Bearing. Contains
small steel balls which
enable the wheel to
move smoothly. Also
situated in the bottom
bracket, pedals and
handlebars.**

The first mountain bikes

In the late 1960s, motorcyclists in
California, USA, were tearing up the
countryside by riding down mountain
trails as spectacularly as possible. This
was soon banned, but
some people were
unrelenting. They
rode down on tough
old bikes instead.

**The indestructible
1930s Schwinn
Excelsior.**

At first, they transported their bikes
uphill in pick-up trucks. But then one
cycling enthusiast, Gary Fisher, fitted
gears to his bike and rode up the steep
Repack Hill. By the late 1970s,
manufacturers were developing bikes
with gears for
off-road use. The
mountain bike boom
had started.

**One of the first
mountain bikes; the
Stumpjumper by
Specialized.**

Road racing bikes

Mountain bikes are designed for
strength and good grip on rough terrain.
In contrast, racing bikes are designed for
lightness and speed on roads.

**Steep angles
provide sensitive
steering.**

**Drop handlebars
for perfect
racing posture.**

**Light
caliper
brakes**

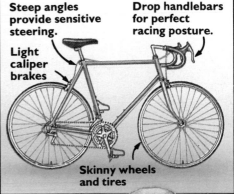

**Skinny wheels
and tires**

Preparing to go

Before setting out, make sure your bike is roadworthy. Some things to look for are described below. Later on in the book, there is advice on how to do simple repairs.

A bike stand is useful, but not essential. If you don't have one, just rest your bike against a wall.

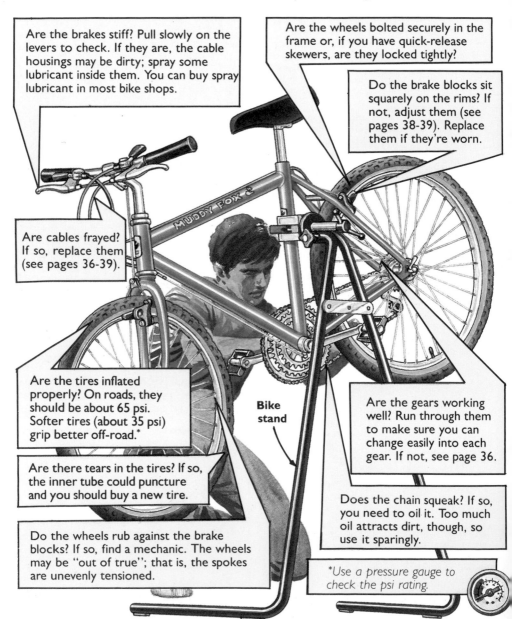

Are the brakes stiff? Pull slowly on the levers to check. If they are, the cable housings may be dirty; spray some lubricant inside them. You can buy spray lubricant in most bike shops.

Are the wheels bolted securely in the frame or, if you have quick-release skewers, are they locked tightly?

Do the brake blocks sit squarely on the rims? If not, adjust them (see pages 38-39). Replace them if they're worn.

Are cables frayed? If so, replace them (see pages 36-39).

Are the tires inflated properly? On roads, they should be about 65 psi. Softer tires (about 35 psi) grip better off-road.*

Bike stand

Are the gears working well? Run through them to make sure you can change easily into each gear. If not, see page 36.

Are there tears in the tires? If so, the inner tube could puncture and you should buy a new tire.

Does the chain squeak? If so, you need to oil it. Too much oil attracts dirt, though, so use it sparingly.

Do the wheels rub against the brake blocks? If so, find a mechanic. The wheels may be "out of true"; that is, the spokes are unevenly tensioned.

*Use a pressure gauge to check the psi rating.

What to wear

Comfortable clothes can make all the difference between an enjoyable ride and a miserable one. Here are some tips.

Shoes

Mountain bike shoes have stiff soles for comfortable and efficient pedaling, and tough uppers. Cheaper alternatives are lightweight hiking boots, or trainers with thick soles.

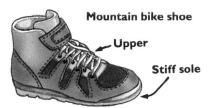

Mountain bike shoe

← **Upper**

Stiff sole

Clothes

Several thin layers are better than one thick one; you can take a layer off if you get hot. Avoid trousers with thick seams in the crotch area.

Cotton or polyester and cotton tops help keep you cool.

Padded cycling gloves protect your hands from blisters and scratches. Make sure they fit snugly.

Shorts made from lycra-spandex are like a second skin, and provide good ventilation. The best sort have a padded crotch lining.

Wool keeps you warm even when it's wet. Polypropylene dries quickly and is a good insulator.
   A windbreaker is essential in cold weather to protect you from the wind.

Basic tool kit

Take the following items along with you on any ride. Wrap them up in a cloth; you can use this to clean your hands after repairs. Tie them behind your saddle or under the top tube.

Small screwdriver   **3, 4, 5 and 6 mm allen keys**

Spare inner tube

Pump   **Adjustable spanner and crank spanner**

Chain tool

Spoke nipple tool

Tire levers

Puncture repair kit   **Pliers**   **Swiss army knife**

Helmets

Most helmets are made of polystyrene, with a plastic and lycra coating. All good ones undergo severe tests for strength and are labelled accordingly.
   Make sure your helmet fits securely and does not interfere with your vision. Test this by putting the helmet on and shaking your head around. It should not flop around or fall forwards.

Bright helmet for city riding.

Learning the basics

Good braking and gear-changing techniques are essential. Once you have mastered them, you can learn the advanced maneuvers covered later in this book with greater confidence and control.

A correct riding position is also important. The pictures below show the most efficient and comfortable positions.

Relax your hands and arms.

Bend your arms slightly.

Put the balls of your feet on the pedals.

As you go faster, tuck down and lean forward.

Keep your hands shoulder-width apart.

Braking

Bad braking techniques could cause you to skid and lose control. Below are the safest techniques. If you feel the bike start to skid, release the front brake.

In wet weather, water between the rims and brake blocks can stop the brakes from working immediately. Because of this, start braking much earlier.

On-road technique

Here you use the front brake as the major force; this prevents the bike from skidding.

1. Put pressure on the front brake, then pull on the back brake, too.

2. Increase the pressure on both brakes until the bike stops.

Off-road technique

Here skidding is more likely. A rear wheel skid is easier to control, so you use mainly the back brake.

1. Keeping your weight as far back as possible, ease on the back brake.

2. Make gentle pulls on the front brake (this is called feathering).

Changing gear

Good use of the gears helps you keep the same pedal rate (cadence) throughout the ride. Ideally, this should be 80-90 revolutions per minute; quite a brisk pace.

You have three ranges of gears, as shown below.

The low range consists of the small chainwheel and the two or three largest sprockets. You use these for climbing hills.

The high range is the large chainwheel and the two or three smallest sprockets. These are for fast conditions.

The closer the chain is to the frame of the bike, the lower the gear you're in.

The middle range of gears is used when you are riding up easy hills or when you are cycling into strong winds.

Gear-changing tips

★ Don't use the large chainwheel with the large sprocket, or the small chainwheel with the small sprocket. These are called the cross-over gears. The chain angle is too steep.

★ Ease off the pressure on the pedals when you change gear. This isn't so important in high speed conditions.

★ Use higher gears for cycling on-road than off-road.

Falling off

If you ride carefully, you may never fall. However, if it does happen, you can reduce the chance of hurting yourself if you try to control the fall as shown on the right.*

The key is to keep relaxed. If you are stiff, your body will absorb the full impact of the fall.

I. Imagine yourself cycling at a fast pace (about 20 kmph or 12 mph). The ground ahead of you appears to be free of obstacles.

2. Suddenly you see a large rock in your way. You abruptly turn the handlebars to the left, but your body keeps going forward.

3. You release your right foot and hand and use them to steady your fall. You use your left ones to ease the bike to the ground.

4. Keeping your arms and legs relaxed to absorb the shock of the fall, you bring your body to a sitting position. No harm is done.

Remember to always wear a helmet.

*Don't attempt this unless the fall is unavoidable.

Turning

Mountain bikes are designed for smooth, easy steering. This means that if you use your body-weight correctly, you can master tight curves with ease. However, it is still a good idea to practice turning in flat, quiet areas before facing heavy traffic or bumpy ground.

The basic turn

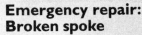

1. Approach the turn with just enough speed to stop you from wobbling.

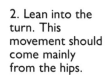

2. Lean into the turn. This movement should come mainly from the hips.

Emergency repair: Broken spoke

1. Remove the wheel and, if it is the back wheel, the freewheel (see page 41).

2. Notice how the broken spoke is threaded through the other spokes. Now unscrew the nipple with a nipple tool and remove the broken spoke.

3. Thread the new spoke on the wheel. Screw in the nipple and tighten it. If necessary, replace the freewheel and back wheel.

4. Spin the wheel. If it hits the brake blocks every so often, tighten the nipple a little more.

Note: If you don't have a spoke with you, just remove the broken one and ride on. Replace it when you get home.

3. Now turn the handlebars as smoothly as you can.

4. Bring the handlebars and your body level again, back on a straight course.

Practising turning

Build a course of large rocks about ten feet apart. Now weave between them, varying the speed and sharpness of the turn. Notice that the faster you go, the more you have to lean into the turn.

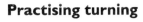

See how slowly you can go.

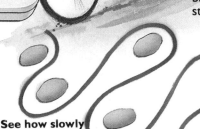

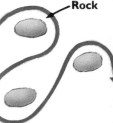

Rock

Sharp turns

If you come across an obstacle unexpectedly, you may need to make a really quick twist around it. The technique below is a good way to do this.

1. Quickly turn the handlebars towards the obstacle, that is, in the opposite direction to the way you want to turn.

2. Immediately turn the handlebars in the direction you want to go. You will be able to make a much sharper turn.

3. When you have passed the obstacle, readjust the handlebars and use your body-weight to coax the bike back on course.

1. Keep up your speed and momentum as you approach the turn.

2. For a left-hand turn, keep the left pedal up as high as it will go.

3. Lean to the left, and push down hard on the right pedal. Gently pull on the back brake.

4. The back wheel will now skid to the right, and try to come round to the front.

Broadslides

Broadslides are performed at moderate to high speeds, and are difficult. Don't try them if you are at all unsure of your ability to control the bike at these speeds.

Because they rely on the bike skidding, you must do them on surfaces with poor traction (grip), such as gravel, grass or dirt. For your first attempts, choose a grassy surface which is free of obstacles.

Although spectacular, this turn can give the impression of irresponsible riding. Don't do it where it may annoy others, or tear up the ground.

5. To counteract the back wheel skid, turn the front wheel gently to the right.

6. Continue leaning to the left and turning the handlebars to the right until the turn is complete.

Going uphill

Riding to the top of a very steep hill is extremely satisfying, and worth all the effort. The advice below will help get you there.

Climbing technique

On steep hills, you should stay in the seat for as long as possible. Your tires cannot grip the surface as well if you stand, and you may lose momentum. However, on a long, gentle hill you may prefer a variety of sitting, standing and honking (see below).

Sitting position: lean forward for more controlled steering.

Standing position: concentrate your weight over the pedals.

Honking position: while standing, use your weight to tip the bike from side to side.

Uphill gear-changing

Ideally, you should keep pedaling at the same rate throughout your climb. To do this, choose lower gears than you can manage, and change down before you have to.

Changing gear under pressure could break the gear mechanisms or cause the chain to fall off. The rear gear is particularly sensitive. To avoid this, pedal faster for a short distance, then ease off the pressure as you change up or down.

Tips

★ Look out for rough patches or obstacles, and steer around them.
★ Change up a gear for standing or honking.
★ Rest your hands on the grips whenever possible. This stops your arms and hands getting overtired.
★ If the back wheel starts to slip, slide back on the saddle.
★ If the front wheel lifts up, sit further forward, or stand and lean forward.
★ If you have both front and back wheel problems, sit further back but lean forward.
★ For cycling on rough terrain where the tires find it difficult to grip, let a little air out of them.

Carrying your bike

Some hills are too much for anyone to master. In these cases you may need to push or carry your bike before you can get in the saddle again. The following technique is the most efficient and energy-saving way to carry your bike.

Top tube over right shoulder.

Hold the left handlebar.

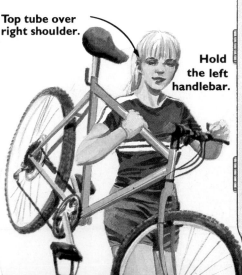

Using toe-clips

Many people use toe-clips for climbing. Keep them fairly loose until you are used to them so you can release your feet more easily if you fall.

Pros	Cons
★ It is easy for your feet to slip when you are climbing. Toe-clips secure them to the pedals.	★ You can't use your feet to help you balance, although you can learn to balance without them.
★ They give you extra pedaling power.	★ If you fall, you may not be able to release your feet before you hit the ground.
★ They help you to pedal evenly.	

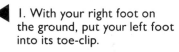

1. With your right foot on the ground, put your left foot into its toe-clip.

2. As you move off, position your right foot on its pedal with the toe-clip underneath.

3. Flick the right pedal over, and slide your foot into the toe-clip.

Emergency repair: Broken chain

1. Use the chain tool to remove one complete link and the pin of the broken link.

2. Snap the ends of the chain together.

3. Push the pin through with the chain tool, bending the chain slightly if the link is stiff.

Note: If the whole chain is worn, buy a new one.

Going downhill

One of the most exhilarating experiences on a mountain bike is riding down a steep slope at full speed. However, at very fast speeds you could seriously hurt yourself, or others, if you lose control. For this reason, never ride recklessly or irresponsibly.

Downhill posture

The trick is to keep your weight low and to the back of the bike, as shown below. Lowering the saddle position will help you to do this (see page 35).

If you lean forward, you are likely to be catapulted over the handlebars.

Before setting off, check your brakes, and make sure your tires are firm.

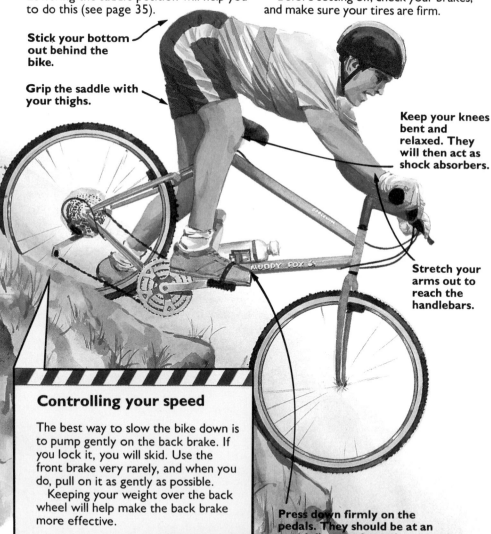

Stick your bottom out behind the bike.

Grip the saddle with your thighs.

Keep your knees bent and relaxed. They will then act as shock absorbers.

Stretch your arms out to reach the handlebars.

Controlling your speed

The best way to slow the bike down is to pump gently on the back brake. If you lock it, you will skid. Use the front brake very rarely, and when you do, pull on it as gently as possible.

Keeping your weight over the back wheel will help make the back brake more effective.

Press down firmly on the pedals. They should be at an equal distance from the ground.

Steering around obstacles

On a fast downhill stretch, an unexpected obstacle such as a rock or log may make you turn the handlebars too sharply and lose control. If you see something ahead, follow these steps.

1. Try to slow the bike down, pulling gently on both brakes. Keep your weight to the back of the bike.

2. Lean your body in the direction of the turn. Now ease the handlebars around as gently as you can.

3. For maximum ground clearance, position the pedal nearest the obstacle as high as possible.

4. Finally, lean outward to bring the bike level again.

Emergency repair: Punctures

1. Remove the wheel (see page 41). Now, starting opposite the valve, remove one side of the tire from the rim.

2. Remove the inner tube then inflate it. Listen for a hiss or put the tube in water and watch for bubbles. Mark the hole.

3. Use fine sandpaper to roughen area around the hole. Blow away any dust. Spread glue on the area. Leave for two minutes.

4. Stick on the patch then let it dry for three minutes. Check in the tire for grit.

5. Starting with the valve, replace the tube, then the tire, on the rim. Make sure it is tucked in all the way. Pump up the tire.

Mountain bike slalom

Just as skiers sometimes take a zig-zag course (slalom) to go down mountains, this can be a good way to ride down very steep slopes. It enables you to go slower as the descent is less severe.

Use a broadslide (see page 10) to change direction in an emergency.

Take a wide course with plenty of turns. This will slow you down and help you stay in control

Wheelies

A wheelie involves pulling the front wheel in the air and balancing on the back one alone. It is a good way to impress friends as it looks trickier than it really is. It is also useful for getting over obstacles.

The basic technique

Practice the basic wheelie technique on a clear area of soft ground, such as grass. Make sure you wear padded clothing to protect you in case you fall.

◀ 1. Get into a low gear and ride along at an easy pace.

2. Bring your weight directly over the back of the bike. ▶

Emergency repair: Dented rim

1. Remove the wheel (see page 41 to find out how to remove a back wheel). Place it on a flat surface.

2. Use a hammer, rock, or block of wood to flatten the dent. Use your other hand to keep the wheel steady.

3. Reassemble the bike. When you get home, take the wheel to a bike shop. They will do a permanent repair with specialist tools, or replace the whole wheel.

Note: Only do this if the dent is badly affecting the brakes; you could split the rim altogether.

3. Pull the handlebars up and back and push down hard on the ◀ pedals.

4. To recover, ▶ bring your body-weight forward again.

16

Using a wheelie over obstacles

Although top riders can wheelie over obstacles of around three feet, most people are content to master obstacles of around one foot. Practice at first with a small log or rock. Secure it by digging it slightly into the ground. Now position yourself about 150ft away.

1. Slowly ride towards the log in a low gear.

2. Just before you reach the log, stand up and bring your weight back.

3. Now use a wheelie (see left) to pull the front wheel over the log.

4. Bring your weight forward to stop the wheelie from going too far. Pedal hard to pull the back wheel over the log too.

Doing a wheelie uphill

If you do a normal wheelie while going uphill you could well fall backwards. Instead, bend your arms and lower your chest as you lift the handlebars. This is called down-unweighting. It will help you over obstacles on your way up.

Don't try this on a steep hill.

You won't lose much speed, so carry on up the hill afterwards.

Doing a wheelie downhill

This is very difficult. If you don't keep your weight back, you could fly over the handlebars. If you do try one, go to a gentle slope. If you feel you're losing control, try to bring the wheel back down again and gently pull on the brakes to reduce your speed.

Ease the bike back to the ground again very gently.

17

Bunny-hopping

A bunny-hop is an extension of a wheelie. After lifting up the front wheel, you raise the back one too.

You are less likely to damage your bike if you use a bunny-hop to get over obstacles. This is because the back wheel hops over obstacles, rather than hitting them.

◀ 1. Follow the instructions on page 16 to lift the front wheel in the air.

2. Bring your weight forward, while pushing down and back on the pedals. ▶

Bunny-hopping tips

★ Both techniques on this page need lots of practice. Don't worry if you can't master them right away.
★ The key to good bunny-hopping is to shift your weight as abruptly and forcefully as you can.
★ Wearing toe clips makes the double wheel technique much easier.

3. The front wheel will hit the ground and the back wheel will rise. ▶

Double wheel technique

A double wheel bunny-hop is when you lift both wheels off the ground simultaneously. Here is how you do it:

1. Ride along slowly on level ground. Stay out of the saddle, and keep your feet level.

2. Quickly push down on the handlebars and pedals, then pull the whole bike upwards.

▼

▼

4. Start pedaling so that the bike clears the obstacle, then bring your weight back over the center of the bike. ▶

Jumping

Full-scale jumps are fun but dangerous. Protect yourself from potential falls by wearing clothes that are well padded (especially on your knees and elbows) and, as always, a strong helmet.

1. Keep your speed up as you approach the area you want to jump.

2. Take off, then use your weight to balance the bike. Keep all your movements as smooth as possible.

3. If you start to wobble, grip the saddle tightly with your thighs.

An off-road track can be precarious, especially if you haven't ridden it before. For example, the ground could suddenly drop in front of you. Alternatively, you could face a deep ditch. A jump is often the best solution.

Jumping a sudden drop in ground level.

Jumping a deep ditch.

Coping with bomb-holes

Some holes (called bomb-holes) are too big to jump. On the right you can see how to ride through one. This is also a good technique to use when you are going too slowly to jump a ditch.

1. Enter the bomb-hole at speed, with your weight well back. At the bottom, bend your knees, and down-unweight.

2. Pedal fast to gain momentum. As you ascend, stop pedaling and bring your weight forward and up.

4. Use your weight to make the rear wheel land slightly before the front one.

Riding on difficult surfaces

Mountain bikes are designed to cope with extreme conditions, including water, mud, sand, ice and snow. However, you do need to adapt your riding technique in order to stay in control of your bike in these conditions. Below are some tips on how to do this.

Before the crossing

★ Inspect the stream carefully:

1. How deep is it? If it's higher than your bottom bracket, you'll end up swimming rather than riding through it.

2. Are there many boulders? If so, try to find a smoother part of the stream.

3. Is the current strong? If so, don't risk it.

★ Lower the seat of your bike (see page 34). This will make you more stable.

★ Loosen your toe straps. You may need to remove your feet in a hurry if you lose your balance.

★ Make sure all the nuts and bolts are done up tightly.

Crossing water

The secret of crossing shallow streams and creeks is to pedal extra hard so you keep going at a fast speed. Your momentum will then carry you over rocks and other obstacles in your way.

1. Approach the stream as quickly as possible. Lean forwards as you enter.

2. Transfer your weight to the back of the bike. This makes it easier for the front wheel to get over rocks and so on.

3. Keep pedaling all the way through if you can. This will help you keep your balance and momentum.

Mud, snow, sand and ice

Riding on these treacherous surfaces requires a lot of common sense. In particular, keep away from melting ice, and avoid cycling in deep snow (10cm or 4 ins is about the limit). Also, never cycle on these surfaces if there are other vehicles present; they could easily lose control and skid into you.

Make sure you clean your bike thoroughly afterwards (see page 35).

	Potential problems	Preparation	Riding tips
Mud and snow	★ Riding fast enough to avoid sinking. ★ Steering. ★ Skidding when climbing. ★ Mud clogging up parts or gear cables freezing.	★ Protect your eyes with fitted glasses. ★ Use knobby tires inflated to about 35 psi. ★ Take spray lubricant. It may help free frozen gears.	★ Pedal quickly in a low gear. ★ Brake very gently. ★ Steer smoothly. An abrupt turn will cause the front wheel to plough sideways.
Sand	★ Sand on the chain makes it hard to change gear. ★ Sinking. ★ Sand flying in your face.	★ Wear glasses, and wrap a scarf around your face. ★ Don't alter tire pressure or tread; no tires grip sand.	★ Stay in a low gear to avoid sinking. ★ Steer very gently. ★ Distribute your weight evenly across the bike.
Ice	★ Skidding. ★ Parts freezing up. ★ Falling off can cause serious injury. Avoid cycling in ice if possible.	★ Use spray lubricant on frozen parts. ★ Neither tire pressure nor grip make a difference.	★ Go just fast enough to balance. ★ No abrupt moves. ★ If you skid, steer into the skid.

4. Keep your weight over the back wheel as the front wheel climbs out of the stream.

Emergency repair: Loose crank

1. Put the chain on the largest chainwheel. Remove dust cap from the crank.

2. Tighten the bolt by fitting the crank spanner over it and turning clockwise. For leverage, press down on opposite pedal with other hand.

3. Replace the dust cap.

21

Cycling in a city

City cycling presents quite different hazards from those you encounter off-road. These pages will help you prepare for and deal with some of them. Also, ask at your local police station for details about courses on road safety.

You can use smooth tires because traction isn't a problem. These will give you a much more comfortable ride, especially if you pump them up hard.

Getting to know the route

It is important to know where you are going. Trying to map-read at the side of the road or follow signposts *en route* prevents you from concentrating on the traffic.

Before your ride, take the time to study your route on a detailed map. You may find it helpful to write yourself brief notes, then memorize them.

Cycle the route slowly, looking out for danger areas. You will then be fully prepared next time.

* North up City Road
* 4th right Hoskins Street
* To traffic circle — approx 5 miles
  2nd left Park Row
* 3rd left Kestrel Street
* 1st right Cherry Tree Rd.
* 2nd right East Welling Avenue

Coping with fumes

Traffic fumes can make city cycling unpleasant and unhealthy. Because you are close to the exhaust pipes, you breathe in carbon monoxide and other chemicals in a concentrated form. You also inhale more as you are breathing harder and faster than normal.

You could buy a mask, but this will only filter out grit. Try to avoid cycling in rush-hour traffic when fumes are dense, and take back roads when possible.

Dressing to be seen

Because your bike is much smaller and quieter than other traffic, it is essential that you do everything you can to draw attention to yourself. Use your lights whenever visibility is bad, not just at night-time.

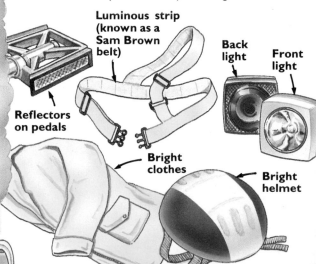

Luminous strip (known as a Sam Brown belt)

Back light

Front light

Reflectors on pedals

Bright clothes

Bright helmet

22

Traffic hazards

Cycling in traffic requires you to cope with situations where other people act stupidly. Below are some things to look out for.

People opening their car doors or pulling out right in front of you.

Motorcyclists (particularly despatch riders) swerving in and out of cars.

Drivers cutting you off as they make a turn into a side road or driveway.

Safety tips

Do:

★ Make clear hand signals.
★ Use a bell, horn or whistle to let others (especially pedestrians) know you're there.
★ Keep looking behind. It's easier to duck your head than twist your neck around.
★ Keep your hands on the brake levers, ready to brake at a moment's notice.
★ Watch out if it starts to rain. The road will be very slippery then and you can lose about 50% of your braking power.
★ Give parked cars a wide berth.

Don't:

★ Jump red or amber traffic lights.
★ Cycle on pavements or the wrong way up one-way streets.
★ Cycle if you have been drinking alcohol. This is dangerous and illegal.
★ Go too slowly; you will frustrate others and make them act stupidly.
★ Cycle too close to the car in front.

Cycling over pot-holes

The best way to deal with pot-holes is to steer around them. However, the flow of traffic may make this impossible. Below you can see how to ride over them safely. Alternatively, do a bunny-hop (see page 18).

1. Slow down, then get into a standing position with your knees bent.

2. Grip the handlebars firmly, keeping your arms relaxed and your weight well back.

3. Keep the bike straight and pull up on the handlebars as you go through the pot-hole.

4. Pick up speed again once the back wheel is clear.

Locking up

You can reduce the chances of your bike being stolen by locking it securely. Take any removeable parts (such as the saddle) with you.

Write your name and address on the bike in indelible ink.

Detach the front wheel (if it is QR) and lock it with the back wheel and frame to a lamp-post, using a steel lock.

Planning an expedition

The secret of a successful cycling trip is thorough planning. Below are some tips on how to prepare for your expedition.

Researching the area

Once you have decided where you would like to go, you need to spend some time finding out what conditions you can expect. As well as making use of guidebooks, there are a number of experts you should talk to.

Question	Who to ask?
1. What will the weather be like? Hot/Cold? Dry/Wet? Humid? Stormy? Windy?	1. Local weather center
2. What sort of extra equipment should I take to cope with the conditions?	2. Local bicycle shop (check cycling magazines for shops in the area).
3. What accommodation is available in the area? Do I need to book in advance?	3. Local tourist office
4. Are there any potential problem areas? Are there any safer routes I could opt for if necessary?	4. Local bicycle shop or a cycling organization (see page 46). They may put you in touch with someone who knows the area.

Packing your bike

You need to keep your bike as light as possible while ensuring you have the essentials. Here are the basics; you may need to take some extras suited to the terrain.

Compass

Matches

Water purification tablets

Paper and pen

Use waterproof pannier bags, or a small back pack.

First aid kit (see page 30)

Spare batteries for your bike lights

Change of clothes

Map

Emergency tool kit (see page 7)

Whistle

Drink bottles

Training

It is a mistake to start cycling very long distances without a proper build-up.

Adapt the basic training program shown below to suit your capabilities.

	WEEK 1	WEEK 2		WEEK 3	WEEK 4
MON	5 miles easy	7 miles easy	MON	10 miles easy	15 miles easy
TUES	5 miles easy	7 miles easy	TUES	10 miles easy	15 miles hard
WED	7 miles easy	7 miles easy	WED	10 miles easy	15 miles easy
THURS	7 miles easy	7 miles easy	THURS	10 miles hard	15 miles hard
FRI	5 miles easy	10 miles easy	FRI	10 miles easy	15 miles easy
SAT	15 miles easy	20 miles easy	SAT	30 miles easy	40 miles easy
SUN	OFF	OFF	SUN	OFF	OFF

Roof-rack or boot-rack?

If you want to transport your bike by car, you will need a bike rack.

Roof-racks can carry up to five bikes. You can buy attachments which enable them to carry other sports gear. They are expensive.

Most **boot-racks** can carry two bikes. They are easier to use, and a fraction of the price.

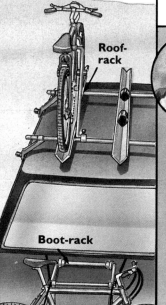

Roof-rack

Boot-rack

Going abroad

If you plan to go abroad, ask a travel agent whether you need any visas. Also find out whether you need medical supplies such as diarrhea tablets, or if you should have any injections.

As well as learning some of the language, find out about the local customs. It is easy to cause offence through the way you dress or behave.

25

The expedition itself

Even the most well-planned expedition could become a total disaster if you don't look after yourselves and each other on the way. These two pages will provide you with some useful advice.

Cycling as a team

It is vital that the stronger cyclists in the group watch out for the weaker ones and alter their riding pace if it is necessary. Use the tips on the right to make sure the whole group works well together.

Food and drink

In the first few hours of cycling, your energy comes from glycogen stored in the muscles and liver. Your body makes glycogen from carbohydrates in food. There are many good sources of carbohydrates; a few are shown below. By eating them before and during the trip, you can improve your cycling performance dramatically.

Fresh vegetables

— **Fresh fruit**

Rice

Pasta

On-ride snacks

"The bonk" is a common problem. It happens when you have used up your glycogen, and have no energy left. To avoid this, eat snacks (such as energy bars or dried fruit) regularly *en-route*.

Energy bars are packed with carbohydrates. Buy them from cycle shops.

You can use up a lot of liquid through sweating. Drink frequently so you don't get dehydrated.

Team tips

★ Work out a realistic plan for the day which you are all happy with. Be ready to alter it if someone gets tired.
★ Put a strong cyclist at the back of the group. It is demoralizing for a slow cyclist to struggle at the back.
★ Don't wait for someone to admit they're tired. They may not want to hold up the rest of the group.
★ If you are cycling into a strong wind, take turns at the front of the group.
★ If you have touring gear, the strongest cyclist should carry the heavier items.

Safety tips

★ Check your equipment daily (see page 6) and listen for rattles or squeaks en-route.
★ Always wear a shirt; riding without one speeds up dehydration.
★ Let someone know your plans each day. Contact them again in the evening when you have arrived safely.
★ If you are hit by very bad weather, take the shortest route to civilization and ask for help. If visibility is bad, find a sheltered place and stay put.

If it is cold, huddle together.

Weather watch

By watching out for rain, you can take shelter before it arrives. Listen to the forecast before you set off, and look for the tell-tale signs below. If you do get drenched, change into dry clothes immediately. If it is very cold, put wet items in a plastic bag at the bottom of your sleeping bag to stop them freezing.

Red sky first thing in the morning.

Low clouds which haven't cleared by midday.

Cumulonimbus clouds mean storms are coming.

Lightning

The metal in your bike attracts lightning and is potentially very dangerous. If you get caught in a lightning storm, abandon your bike and head for shelter. Avoid high ground or trees; lightning looks for the shortest route to earth, and either of these may be its target.

Entering a competiton

You don't have to be a top rider to enter a mountain bike competition. Unlike road racing, you are competing against the terrain just as much as against other cyclists. It is a perfect opportunity to watch others and pick up tips from them.

You can often enter just by turning up on the day. However, many races have number restrictions, so it is safer to send off an entry form in advance. These are available from the race organization, bike shops and magazines.

Types of competition

There are four main types of competition, described below.

Cross-country racing. Competitors race over a course which contains sharp turns, obstacles to jump, streams, steep hills and so on. The cyclist who gets to the finish line first is the winner.

Downhills and slalom. Cyclists ride at top speed down a hair-raising hill. The start is normally staggered (that is, riders start one at a time). The cyclist with the best time wins.

Hill-climbs. Cyclists climb a steep hill, negotiating rocks, loose dirt and so on. Normally a staggered start, the winner is either the one with the best time, or who climbs the highest.

Observed trials. Competitors ride over obstacles, watched by judges. The aim is to get no points. You score one if you touch the ground (dab), three for numerous dabs and five for a fall or a stop.

Preparing to race

Three main things affect your racing performance: your fitness, energy, and the condition of your bike. By concentrating on improving each of these, you will greatly increase your chances of success.

1. Fitness. How fit you are largely depends on your training schedule. Aim to include both long-distance road cycling (for endurance) and off-road challenges, such as climbing and jumping (for strength and technique).

2. Energy. This largely depends on your diet. You can build up your energy stores by eating food which is high in carbohydrates (see page 26). To preserve your energy, only train lightly the day before the race.

3. Bike. If anything goes wrong with your bike during a race, you must fix it on your own. It is vital that you check your bike at least a day before the race, and carry a puncture repair kit and pump during the race.

Race day tips

If you are allowed to, pre-ride the course to get familiar with the difficult parts. Then at least you'll know what to expect.

START

Try to get a good start (if it is a mass start, the front bikes kick up mud and dust on those behind).

If you want to overtake riders, warn them, then wait for them to respond before trying to get past.

You must move over quickly if a racer warns you he or she is about to overtake.

If you get a puncture, fix it and get going as quickly as possible. Some people carry small carbon dioxide cartridges with them which inflate the tyre in seconds.

Don't try to be flashy by jumping higher than necessary; the bike is only in control when on the ground.

FINISH

Iditabike

This is one of the most grueling races invented. Cyclists ride a 320km (200 mile) course in Alaska in winter. Temperatures drop to −20°C, giving many riders frostbite and even causing tires to deflate.

Injuries

You can avoid most cycling injuries by taking a few simple precautions. However, the odd ache or scratch is unavoidable; below is advice on how to treat them. For more serious injuries, see your doctor.

Warming up and down

You can often avoid getting aching muscles by doing a few light exercises before and after the ride. This is particularly important before and after a race. Some good ones are shown below.

Always start the ride gently, gradually building up as your muscles loosen. Ease off the pace as you cycle home.

Don't be tempted to coast down hills. By pedaling, you help your muscles to recover from the stress of intense effort, and keep the blood circulating.

Knee lunges: keeping your right leg straight, lunge to the left for ten seconds. Go back to the standing position, then lunge to the right. Repeat five times.

Arm rotations: Stretch your arms out on either side of you. Now rotate them forward ten times, then backwards ten times. Repeat five times.

Toe touches: With feet apart and legs straight, touch your left foot with your right hand, then your right foot with your left hand. Do ten times.

First aid kit

Aim to include at least the following items in your kit:

★ Large triangular bandage (for slings)
★ Sterile dressings
★ Roll of bandage
★ Elastic bandage
★ Bandaid
★ Aspirin
★ Antiseptic lotion
★ Cleansing wipes
★ Insect repellant
★ Scissors
★ Tweezers
★ Safety pins

Making an ice pack

You can relieve an aching limb by holding an ice pack against it for about 20 minutes. You can buy ice packs from large pharmacies. Alternatively, use a packet of frozen peas, or make a home-made ice pack shown below. Always keep a towel between the ice pack and limb to avoid ice burns.

Alcohol prevents the mixture from freezing.

1. Mix together some water and medicinal alcohol (available from pharmacies).

2. Pour into a container. Label it.

3. Put in the freezer. When you need it, pour into a waterproof bag.

Injury chart

Problem	Cause	Solution
Stiff neck	Wearing a heavy helmet, lack of head movement, or over-stretched riding position.	Rotate your head from time to time or buy a lighter helmet. Lower saddle or move it forwards (see page 35).
Stitch	Lack of oxygen getting to muscles, and overworking the diaphragm through quick, shallow breathing.	Reduce cycling pace. Practice taking deeper breaths from the abdomen rather than the chest.
Blisters or numb hands	Gripping the handlebars too tightly or too much weight on the wrists because handlebars are too low or too far forward.	Wear padded cycling gloves or use a more padded grip. Vary hand position on long rides. Adjust handlebars (see pages 44-45).
Stiff knees	Cycling in too high a gear, or for too long. Alternatively, a too low or high saddle.	Reduce gear and build up distance gradually. Set seat to proper height (see page 35).
Numb feet	Wearing tight shoes, or using tight toe straps.	Buy new shoes, or loosen toe straps.
Cramp	Cycling too hard without proper training, or not drinking enough.	Gently rub area. Build up cycling distances/intensity gradually. Drink regularly when cycling.
Aching buttocks	Using a hard saddle, or cycling too far without a build-up.	Buy a new saddle or wear padded trousers or shorts.
Cuts and scratches	On-ride falls or scrapes	Clean with running water then disinfect. Stop a deep cut from bleeding by dressing it tightly, and covering with a thick bandage.
Sprain or pulled muscle	Falling or moving awkwardly	Press an ice-pack against it, then bandage and rest.
Headache, light-headedness or wheezy chest.	Dehydration	Stop cycling, and drink fluid. Rest in the shade and if you have enough water, pour some on your head.

Buying a mountain bike

There are so many mountain bikes on the market that it is easy to get confused when buying one. Below is advice on how to make sure you end up with a bike that is good value and will last you for some time.

Finding a good shop

If you decide to buy a brand-new bike, it is worthwhile to look for a good specialist shop that will not only give you sound advice on your purchase, but will also supply you with back-up mechanical help when you need it. Go to several shops, preferably when they are not too busy (winter is ideal). Look out for the following things:

★ Do they have a good selection?
★ Are the salespeople answering their customers' questions intelligently and courteously? Are they pushy?

★ How do the prices compare with other shops?
★ Do they have a service area with mechanics who can modify bikes to suit their customers' needs?
★ Do they offer free services with the purchase of a bike, such as a year's free maintenance?

Don't consider buying a bike from any shop which fails to impress you on all these counts. Also, ask friends and neighbors whether the shop has a good reputation.

Narrowing it down

To narrow down your choice of bikes, you need to ask yourself the following questions:

★ Will I ride it mostly on- or off-road?
★ What is my price limit?
★ Do I want to race on it?

The test ride

Now take your favorite bike for a short ride in a quiet area. Do the following tests:

★ If you can, take both hands off the handlebars. Does the bike continue in a straight line?
★ Try out all the gears. Are the changes smooth?

★ Try a few emergency stops. How good are the brakes?
★ Does the bike fit you; do you feel cramped, or are you reaching for the handlebars and pedals (see right)?

Before making a decision to buy the bike, take out a few other bikes for test rides to compare their performances.

The final adjustments

The salesperson should now fine-tune the bike to make it perfect for you. This includes getting the fit right, and adding any accessories that you want.

Buying second-hand

Used bikes can be excellent value for your money if you know what to look for. It is worth getting the advice of an experienced rider or mechanic before putting your money on the table. Also, check the cost of similar new bikes to make sure the second-hand price is reasonable.

Places to look

1. Phone local bike shops to find out whether they stock used bikes. Many overhaul used bikes, and sell them with a guarantee.

2. Check bike shops for notice boards. These often advertise used bikes.
3. Look in the classified sections of cycling magazines.

Inspecting the bike

A used bike is bound to have taken some knocks in its time. However, you should look out for major signs of damage or wear such as those described below.
If you are confident that the bike is roadworthy, take it for a test ride.

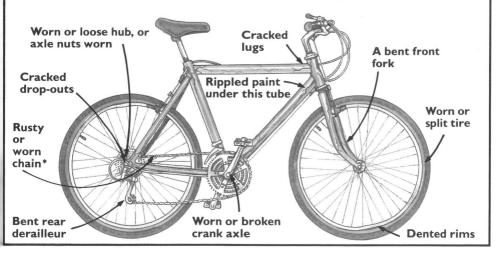

- Worn or loose hub, or axle nuts worn
- Cracked lugs
- A bent front fork
- Cracked drop-outs
- Rippled paint under this tube
- Worn or split tire
- Rusty or worn chain*
- Bent rear derailleur
- Worn or broken crank axle
- Dented rims

Checking the fit

When you buy a second-hand bike, you alone are responsible for making sure it fits you correctly. Check the following:

1. Are the seatpost and handlebar stem long enough for you to set the saddle and handlebars at the right height?**
2. Straddle the bike. For city riding, there should be at least 3-5cm (1-2 ins) between your crotch and top tube; twice that for off-road riding.

3. Can you reach the handlebars while keeping your elbows slightly bent?

Never buy a bike that doesn't fit you:

★ Low handlebars make you lean too far forward, causing a stiff neck and sore back.
★ A badly-positioned saddle can give you knee, hip and ankle problems.
★ If the top tube is too high, you could get very painful injuries in a fall.

---

*This will mean replacing the chainwheels and sprockets as well as the chain.
**See pages 35 and 45 for more about this.

If you want to get the most out of your bike, you need to take good care of it. The following twelve pages will help you do just that.

Don't worry if many of the parts shown in the photographs aren't exactly the same as those on your bike. There are lots of different makes and models of bike, but they all work in a similar way.

Cleaning your bike

Cleaning your bike stops mud from building up, and makes it run better. It also lets you inspect the bike more closely. After a muddy ride, give it a quick clean before the mud has time to dry. Clean it thoroughly two or three times a year.

Post-ride clean

You will need:
Garden hose
2 clean old towels
An old, medium-sized paintbrush
Spray lubricant, such as WD40

1. Use the hose and brush to remove mud. Don't jet water at the headset*, bottom bracket** and pedals; dirty water damages the bearings.
2. Wipe the bike. Clean the moving parts and chain with lubricant, avoiding brake blocks and rims.

Thorough clean

You will need:
Garden hose
2 buckets
1 shallow metal tray
2 sponges
3 rags or old towels
1 stiff brush
1 soft brush
Liquid detergent
Tooth brush
Kerosene *
Good quality car wax *
Piece of wire wool (medium texture) *
Chain tool **
Chain oil **
Touch-up paint **
Spray lubricant *
Spanner (if wheels aren't QR)

* Available from a hardware store
** Available from a bicycle shop.

1. Spray off most of the mud with a hose.
2. Place your bike on a repair stand, or place it upside-down on a flat area. Use a towel to protect it from scuffs.
3. Remove the wheels (see page 40).
4. Break the chain with a chain tool (see page 13), put it in a shallow tin, and cover with kerosene. Use the toothbrush to scrub off the worst grime, then replace the dirty kerosene with clean. Leave the chain soaking.
5. Wipe the chainwheels with a towel, then clean the freewheel sprockets with the firm brush.
6. Turn the frame the right side up, and rest it on the front forks and chainwheels.
7. Mix detergent and hot water in a bucket. Clean the frame and wheels with this, using the soft brush. Rinse with a hose, avoiding the bearing parts (see above).
8. Remove any rust from the frame with wire wool. Touch up with paint and allow several hours to dry.
9. Rub wax into the frame, then polish it off when dry.
10. Hold the chain above the tray, and let the spirit drip from it until it's dry.
11. Turn the frame upside-down again and replace the wheels. Put the chain on and join with a chain tool.
12. With the bike the right side up, spray lubricant on the chain, gears and brake pivots. Avoid getting any on the rims or blocks, or the brakes won't work.

*See page 44.
**See page 42.

Checking the saddle height

A badly-positioned saddle can cause you a great deal of pain (see page 31). Do the following test to see if you need to alter the height of your saddle.

Using a wall to help you balance, sit on the bike and position the pedal at its lowest position. Now put your foot on it. Your leg should be slightly bent (see right).

Correct height   Incorrect height

Adjusting the height

The way you adjust the saddle height depends on whether you have a quick-release or bolt-on saddle. In either case,

you should leave at least 6.5cm (2.5 ins) of stem inside the frame so it is held securely.

Quick-release (QR) saddles: open the QR lever and raise or lower the saddle. If it's stiff, twist it at the same time. Close the QR lever and check that it's tight.

QR lever

Binder bolt

Bolt-on saddles: use a spanner or allen key to undo the binder bolt. Raise or lower the saddle, twisting it as you do so if it's stiff. Tighten the binder bolt firmly.

Tool kit

To do the maintenance repairs covered on the next few pages, you will need the following items:

Screwdrivers

Brake cables
Gear cables
Spoke nipple tool
Allen keys

Plastic-ended hammer

Pliers
Cable cutters
Torch

Spray lubricant

Spare brake blocks

Bearings
Hook spanner
Bicycle grease

Adjustable spanner
Pin tool

Rags

Tire levers
Chain tool
Cotterless crank removing tool
Headset spanner
Freewheel remover
Cone spanner
Small spanner

Maintenance tips

★ Good tools last longer and make the job easier. To save money, buy jointly with a friend.
★ Clean tools with a rag when you have finished, and store them in a box.
★ Spread paper under the bike to soak up oil or catch dirt.
★ Whenever you dismantle a part, lay out the pieces in the order they came off, and watch carefully so that you can reassemble it correctly.
★ Study your owner's manual (if you have one) before starting.
★ Look up unfamiliar technical terms in the glossary on page 47.

There is nothing more frustrating than trying to get up a hill, only to find that your gears fail you. Skillful gear-changing and regular maintenance will help prevent this from happening.

Derailleur height

Put the chain on the middle chainwheel. There should be $1/16$in between the outer plate of the front derailleur and the teeth of the largest chainwheel.

If the front derailleur is too high or low, it may not control the chain effectively. Correct this by loosening the clamp bolt and moving the derailleur up or down. Retighten the bolt firmly.

How they work

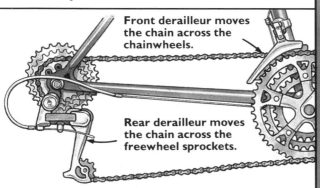

Front derailleur moves the chain across the chainwheels.

Rear derailleur moves the chain across the freewheel sprockets.

The derailleurs do just what they say they do: they derail the chain. When you move the right gear lever, the rear derailleur shifts the chain from one freewheel sprocket to another. When you move the left gear lever, the front derailleur moves the chain from one chainwheel to another.

Derailleur alignment

Sometimes a derailleur gets knocked so that it sits at an angle to the sprockets or chainwheels. This stops it from working smoothly and efficiently. Check both derailleurs regularly, particularly after a bad fall, and if necessary correct them as follows:

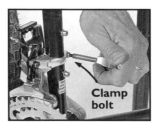

Clamp bolt

If the rear derailleur isn't aligned with the freewheel sprockets, gently pull it into position with a large adjustable spanner.

If the front derailleur isn't aligned, undo the clamp bolt. Reset derailleur then retighten the bolt while holding the derailleur.

Replacing a cable

When a cable starts to fray or rust, it is a sure sign that it will snap before long. If you inspect your cables regularly, and replace them when necessary, you can avoid the possibility of one snapping just when you most need it.

If one gear cable looks worn, think about replacing the other one too. It is probably coming to the end of its life.

Notice that the cable is made up of an inner wire running through a flexible plastic casing (housing).

Overshifting and undershifting

A common derailleur problem is that the chain overshoots the smallest or largest sprocket or chainwheel. This is called overshifting. Alternatively, it may be impossible to move the chain into the smallest or largest sprocket or chainwheel. This is undershifting.

There are two screws on the rear derailleur, called the high and low adjustment screws. These control how far the derailleur moves the chain across the sprockets when you change gear.

At the top of the front derailleur are the inside and outside limit screws. These control how far the derailleur moves the chain across the chainwheels.

Rear derailleur

Turn high adjustment screw* clockwise if the chain overshoots the small sprocket. Turn anti-clockwise if the chain won't go into it.

Turn low adjustment screw* clockwise if the chain overshoots the large sprocket. Turn anti-clockwise if the chain won't go into it.

Front derailleur

Turn inside limit screw** clockwise if the chain overshoots the small chainwheel. Turn it anti-clockwise if it won't go into the small chainwheel.

Turn outside limit screw** clockwise if the chain overshoots the large chainwheel. Turn it anti-clockwise if it won't go into the large chainwheel.

 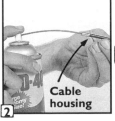  

1 Put the chain on the smallest cog and chainwheel. Notice the route the cable takes. Loosen the cable anchor bolt, pull the gear lever and release it a few times. Pull out the cable wire with pliers.

2 Spray lubricant in the housings, or if they are split, replace them. Now, remembering where the old cable went, thread new cable through the gear lever, cable housing and bottom bracket guide.

3 Thread the new cable through the rear derailleur housing, then through the cable anchor bolt. Pull it tightly by hand or with pliers, then tighten the anchor bolt using a spanner or allen key.

4 Trim off any extra cable. Put a cap on the end of the cable to stop it from fraying. Try out the gears to make sure the cable is secure. Finally, retighten the cable if it goes slack; new cable often stretches.

*Most rear derailleurs have an H and an L to mark the high and low screw.
** The inside screw is the one closest to the frame.

If you want to ride your bike with confidence, you must be certain that your brakes will not fail you when you need them. Never go out on your bike without checking your brakes (see page 6). The steps on these two pages will enable you to overhaul them.

How they work

There is a cable running from each brake lever to the two brake units. Different bikes have different types of brake unit, but most mountain bikes have the tough cantilever brakes shown in the picture below.

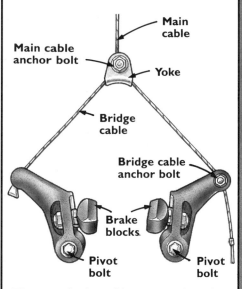

Main cable

Main cable anchor bolt

Yoke

Bridge cable

Bridge cable anchor bolt

Brake blocks

Pivot bolt **Pivot bolt**

The main brake cable is secured to the yoke of the brake unit by a cable anchor bolt. In addition to this, a cable (called a bridge cable or straddle wire) loops through the yoke.

When you pull on the brake lever, the yoke pulls on the brake unit. The unit then pivots, pushing the blocks against the rim of the wheel.

Tensioning the brakes

If the brakes take a long time to respond, or they are rubbing against the rim as you ride, it could be because the brake tension is wrong. To adjust the tension, you will need to ask a friend to help you.

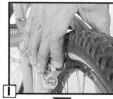

Ask your friend to squeeze the brake blocks as firmly as possible against the rim of the wheel.

Loosen the cable anchor bolt. Pull some cable through or release some, then retighten the bolt.

Ask your friend to let go. Pull on the brake levers a few times to check the tension.

Bridge cable tension

Your bike may have a bridge cable anchor bolt which allows you to alter the tension here instead.

Ask your friend to hold the brake blocks against the rim. Undo the bridge cable anchor bolt.

Release some bridge cable, or pull some through. Retighten the nut and test the brakes as above.

*You may also need to readjust the brake blocks as shown above.

Adjusting the brake blocks

It is important that the whole of each brake block hits the rim. If it is too high, it will damage the tire. If it is too low, it will lose braking power.

To stop it from squeaking, angle it so that the front part hits the rim first. This is called "toeing the brake in".

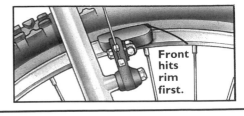

Front hits rim first.

To adjust a brake block, loosen the brake block nut and move the block. Retighten the nut securely.

Replacing a brake block

Worn brake blocks don't work effectively. Replacing them is cheap and easy.

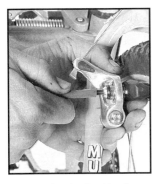

Loosen the brake block nut and ease out the old block. Replace with a new one, positioning it correctly (see above) before tightening the nut.

Replacing a worn brake cable

A worn brake cable is likely to snap when you put a lot of stress on it. For obvious reasons, this is something you want to avoid. Replace brake cables as soon as they start to fray or rust.

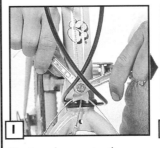

1

Notice the route the cable takes between the anchor bolt and the brake lever. Release one end from the bolt and the other from the lever. Remove from housing.

2

Spray lubricant inside the housing, or replace it if it is cracked. Install a new cable into the brake lever. Pull firmly on the cable and lever to ensure the cable is secure.

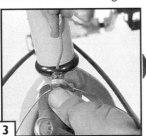

3

Thread the cable into the housing. Remembering the route of the old cable, position the new cable through all the guides along the frame towards the anchor bolt.

4

Slip the cable through the anchor bolt, then loop the bridge cable over the yoke. Finally, adjust the brakes by tensioning the brake or bridge cable as described above.

Do you live in horror of getting a problem in your back wheel, such as a puncture or broken spoke? If so, this is probably because you don't know how to remove or replace the back wheel or freewheel. The following steps will show you how to do this.

How it works

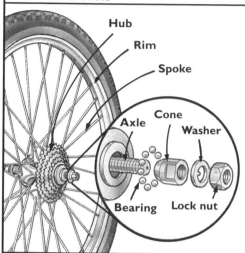

Hub
Rim
Spoke
Cone
Axle
Washer
Bearing
Lock nut

The wheel is made up of a hub and rim, held together by spokes. The spokes must be tensioned correctly for the wheel to rotate evenly. This is a specialist job; have your wheels retensioned by a mechanic if they are buckled.

The hub consists of an axle, a cone, bearings, washers and a lock nut. The bearings allow the wheel to turn while the axle stays still. The axle is fixed in the frame by means of axle nut or a quick-release (QR).

On the back wheel, there is a freewheel. This enables the wheel to rotate forward without turning the rear sprockets and the pedals with it. This means that you can coast along the road without the pedals turning.

Checking the bearings

Sometimes the hub bearings get so full of dirt and grit that they don't work properly. Alternatively, they may become worn and too loose. Check yours as described on the right. If you do find a problem, replace the bearings (see below).

Too tight?

Remove the wheel, and hold it by the axle. Now spin it. It should turn without resistance from the hub.

Too loose?

Hold the wheel by the axle, and rock it from side to side. There should be no sideways movement in the hub.*

Overhauling the hub

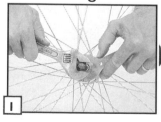

1

2

3

Holding the hub cone with a cone spanner, use an adjustable spanner to take off the lock nut.

Remove the washers, cone and bearings. Remove the axle from the other side of the hub.

Use a wide screwdriver to take out the dust covers gently. Now clean the cone, axle and hub.

*On a QR system, there can be a little movement.

Removing the back wheel

1

With chain in the small sprocket, pull short end of bridge cable to open brake. Open QR or axle nuts.

2

Push the wheel forward and pull the rear derailleur hanger back, as shown in the photo above.*

3

Lift the back of the bike until the wheel falls clear of the chain. Remove the wheel.

Replacing the back wheel

1

Holding the chain with your right hand, position the wheel inside the frame.*

2

Now carefully position the chain on to the teeth of the smallest cog in the freewheel.

3

Slide the axle into the drop-outs, ensuring the wheel is centered. Tighten the QR or axle nuts.

Removing the freewheel

1

Remove the wheel. Put the freewheel remover in the freewheel. Secure it with the QR or axle nut.

2

Put a spanner over the freewheel remover as shown above, then push on it with all your weight.

3

When the freewheel gives, undo the QR or nut and unscrew the freewheel with the remover.**

4

Inspect the cone for pitting. Roll the axle; it will move unevenly if bent. Replace if necessary.

5

Use your fingers to put grease in the hub. Now install the new bearings inside the hub.

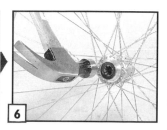

6

Gently tap in the dust covers with a hammer. Reassemble the other parts in reverse order.

*If you don't have a bike stand, you might need someone to hold the bike.

**When you put it back, screw it on firmly by hand. It will tighten itself when you ride.

Maintenance 5: Bottom bracket

Because the bottom bracket is so close to the ground it is an obvious target for any grit, mud, water and so on that is thrown off the front wheel while you are riding. For this reason, it is important that you overhaul it regularly. This is called "repacking the bottom bracket".

How it works

The bottom bracket is really the heart of the bicycle. It contains an axle, fixed in place by two bearings. The two cranks revolve around these bearings when you pedal.

At one end of the axle there is a fixed cup. At the other end is an adjustable cup which allows you to tighten or loosen the movement of the axle. The adjustable cup is held in place by a lock ring.

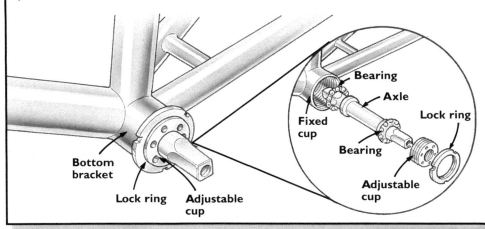

Bottom bracket

Lock ring   Adjustable cup

Bearing
Axle
Fixed cup
Lock ring
Bearing
Adjustable cup

Checking the axle movement

The test on the right will enable you to see whether the axle is too tight or too loose. Generally, you can correct the movement by adjusting the bearings (see far right). Although the photo shows this with the cranks off, you can do it with them on.

You may find that you cannot make the axle any tighter, or make it run smoothly. If so, the bearings are badly worn, and you should replace them when repacking the bottom bracket.

Testing for loose bearings.

Pin tool

Hook spanner

A. Hold each crank by the pedal and rock it. If there is play at the axle, the bearings are too loose.
B. Rest the front of the chain on the bottom bracket and spin the cranks. If you feel resistance, the bearings are too tight.

To adjust the bearings, undo the lock ring and hold it steady with a hook spanner. To make the bearings tighter, screw in the adjustable cup with a pin tool. To loosen, undo the cup slightly. Retighten the lock ring while holding the cup steady.

Removing the cranks

In order to repack the bottom bracket, you need first to remove the cranks.

Pin tool

1

Put the chain on the large chainwheel.* Remove the dust caps. Now, using the crank spanner, remove each nut or bolt and washer.

2

Firmly screw the crank removing tool into one of the cranks. Turn the outside bolt on the tool, holding on to the pedal for leverage.

3

Remove the crank to expose the cup and spindle. Now remove the other crank. Clean the bottom bracket with a rag and spray lubricant.

Repacking the bottom bracket

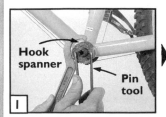

Hook spanner

Pin tool

1

Remove the cranks. Now remove the lock ring on the left side.

Adjustable cup

3

Clean the cup with lubricant, then inspect it. If it's pitted, replace it.

Dust shield

5

If your bike has a dust shield in the bottom bracket shell, remove it.

7

Reassemble the axle parts in reverse order, liberally greasing them.

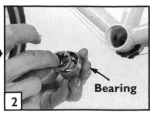

Bearing

2

Carefully remove the adjustable cup with a pin tool. Take out the bearing.

Axle

4

Remove the axle. Now spray it with lubricant and clean it thoroughly.

6

Remove the bearing and fixed cup.** Clean the cup and bottom bracket shell.

8

Tap the cranks on with a hammer. Screw in nuts, then tighten with spanner.

*This stops the teeth cutting your hand if the spanner slips.
**On most bikes, you turn the fixed cup clockwise to remove it.

43

Maintenance 6: Headset

Most steering problems occur because the headset is worn or dirty, or too tight or loose. Follow these steps to overhaul yours.

How it works

The headset is the center of the steering system. It consists of a set of bearings at each end of the head tube. When you turn the handlebars, the headset bearings turn too, enabling the front fork and wheel to move with them.

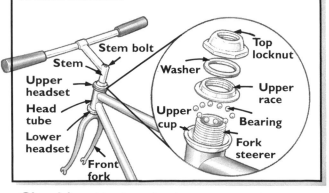

Checking the headset movement

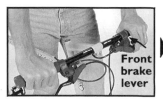

Front brake lever

Hold wheel between legs.

Hold the front brake lever tightly and rock the bike backwards and forwards. There should be no rattling from the front fork or the handlebars.

Problems?

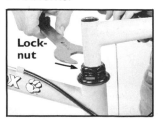

Lock-nut

Pick up the front of the bike and turn the handlebars left and right as far as they will go. They should turn without resistance or binding.

Undo the top locknut. Tighten or loosen the upper race. Retighten the locknut.
  Carry out the tests again and adjust the upper race until it is neither too tight nor too loose.

The overhaul

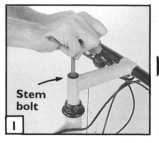

Stem bolt

1

Loosen the stem bolt with a spanner or allen key. Tap the bolt with a plastic hammer or block of wood if necessary.

5

Start unscrewing the upper race. This holds the fork in the frame, so you will have to support the fork from below.

9

Replace the bearing cups and bearings on the fork and headtube. Now fit the front fork back into the frame.

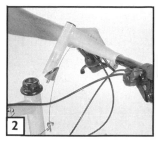

2

Remove the handlebars from the frame (you may have to pull hard). Use a rag to clean any grease and rust from the stem.

3

Allow the handlebars to hang gently to one side of the frame. Make sure they do not bump or scratch the frame.

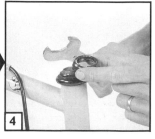

4

Remove the top locknut from the frame, using a spanner. Now remove any washers or reflector brackets.

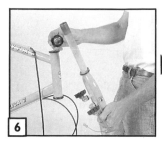

6

Making sure no bearings fall out, remove the upper race from the head tube. Now remove the fork from the frame.

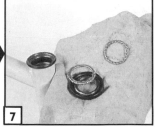

7

Clean all parts including the fork and inside the frame. Look at the races: if they're worn or pitted, replace the headset.

8

Next, rub a generous amount of new grease into the bearing cups and bearings with the tips of your fingers.

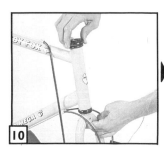

10

Screw the upper race on to the head tube until it is just hand-tight. Put the washers and brackets back in the right order.

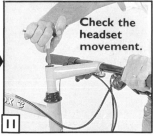

Check the headset movement.

11

Holding the upper race with a spanner, replace the lock nut. Fit the handlebars at the correct height (see right).

Handlebar height

The handlebars can be positioned anywhere between the height of the saddle and 5cm (2 ins) below it, depending on which you find most comfortable.

Always keep at least 5cm of stem in the head tube to ensure it doesn't break. If 5cm line isn't marked, do it yourself with an indelible pen.

Going further

Joining a mountain bike organization is a very good way to get the best out of the sport. Many provide you with information on competitions, routes, books and so on. Some fight on your behalf to keep tracks open to cyclists and improve the image of mountain bike riding as a sport. Nearly all of them support local clubs and put you in touch with enthusiasts in your area.

Great Britain

The Rough Stuff Fellowship
9 Liverpool Avenue
Ainslie
Southport
Lancashire PRB 3NE
GB

The Mountain Bike Club
1 Santon House
Santon
Downham
Suffolk IP7 OTT
GB

The British Cyclo-Cross Association
59 Jordan Road
Sutton Coldfield
West Midlands, B75 5AE
GB

USA

Bikecentennial
PO Box 8308
Missoula, MT 59807
USA

LAW (League of American Wheelmen)
Suite 209
6707 Whitestone Road
Baltimore, MD 21207
USA

NORBA (National Off-Road Bicycling Association)
1750 E. Boulder
Colorado Springs
CO 80909
USA

Canada

Canadian Cycling Association
1600 prom. James Naismith Drive
Gloucester
Ontario
Canada KIB 5N4

Ontario Cycling Association
1220 Sheppard Ave. E.
Willowdale
Ontario
Canada M2K 2XI

WORCA (Whistler Off-Road Cycling Association)
Box 796
Whistler, B.C.
Canada VON 180

Australia

Australian Mountain Bike Association
P.O. Box N25
Grosvenor Place
Sydney, NSW 2000
Australia

New Zealand

New Zealand Mountain Bike Association
PO Box 388 Waikato Mail Centre
Hamilton
New Zealand

International

International Mountain Bike Association
Route 2, Box 303
Bishop, CA 93514
USA

Glossary

Adjustable cup A threaded **bearing cup** which controls the adjustment of the bottom bracket bearings.

Allen key A six-sided, L-shaped tool used on certain bolts.

Axle A rod around which the cranks or hubs rotate.

Bearing cup A cylindrical holder which contains steel balls and grease. The **axle** rotates on the steel balls.

Binder bolt Bolt which holds the seatpost in place.

Brake blocks The rubber blocks in the brake that rub against the rim when the brake is on.

Chain tool A tool for breaking apart or rejoining a chain. It does this by pushing a pin in or out.

Cone spanner A spanner that is very thin so it can fit hub cones.

Cotterless crank removing tool A device that screws into a crank and pulls it off the axle.

Crank spanner A spanner that tightens the bolt or nut which holds the crank on to the bottom bracket **axle.**

Drop-outs The slots on the frame inside which the front and back wheel are clamped.

Dust cap A threaded cover that screws into the crank. It protects the bolt and washer that hold the crank on the **axle.** It also protects the threads which the **cotterless crank removing tool** screws into.

Dust shield A cover that keeps dust out of the bearings.

Fixed cup A threaded **bearing cup** which holds the bottom bracket **axle** and bearings on the chainwheel side.

Freewheel remover A tool that fits into the freewheel and, with the aid of a spanner, removes the freewheel from the hub.

Hook spanner A spanner used to loosen or tighten the **lock ring** on the bottom bracket bearings.

Inner tube Rubber tube which fits inside a tire and holds the air when you pump it up.

Lock ring A threaded ring which screws on to the **adjustable cup** and prevents it from coming loose.

Pin tool A tool with two pins on a Y-shaped spanner used for turning the **adjustable cup** on the bottom bracket.

Pressure gauge A device that measures the air pressure in the tire when you press it on to the tire **valve**.

psi Pounds per square inch. Unit of measurement used to indicate the amount of air pressure in a tire. The metric measurement is atmospheres, but most manufacturers usually use the non-metric psi units.

Race A circular metal ring that is used as a track for ball bearings to roll on.

Spoke nipple tool A small hand-held spanner that fits on to the spoke nipple. It is used to increase or decrease spoke tension between the rim and hub.

Tire lever A plastic or metal lever used to remove the tire from the rim.

Valve The device on an **inner tube** through which air is pumped or released.

Index